Children of the World

South Korea

For their help in the preparation of *Children of the World: South Korea*, the editors gratefully thank Chung Ho Chung, the University of Wisconsin-Milwaukee; the Embassy of the Republic of Korea (Canada), Ottawa, Ont.; the Embassy of the Republic of Korea (US), Washington, DC; the International Institute of Wisconsin, Milwaukee; the United States Department of State, Bureau of Public Affairs, Office of Public Communication, Washington, DC, for unencumbered use of material in the public domain; the Canadian Department of Employment and Immigration, Ottawa, Ont.; the US Immigration and Naturalization Service, Press Office, Washington, DC.

Library of Congress Cataloging-in-Publication Data

Kubota, Makoto.
   South Korea : photography.

   (Children of the world)
   "Original text . . . by Yumiko Takada"—T.p. verso.
   "Originally published in shortened form consisting of section 1 only"—T.p. verso.
   Bibliography: p.
   Includes index.
   Summary: Introduces the culture of South Korea by depicting the life of an eleven-year-old resident of Seoul who is preparing for a career as an athlete.
   1. Korea (South)—Juvenile literature. 2. Children—Korea (South)—Juvenile literature. [1. Korea (South)]

I. Tolan, Sally. II. Knowlton, MaryLee, 1946–
III. Sachner, Mark, 1948–   IV. Takada, Yumiko.
V. Title. VI. Series: Children of the world (Milwaukee, Wis.)
DS922.2.K83 1987   951.9'043   86-42804
ISBN 1-55532-193-3
ISBN 1-55532-168-2 (lib. bdg.)

North American edition first published in 1987 by

Gareth Stevens, Inc.
7317 West Green Tree Road Milwaukee, Wisconsin 53223, USA

Typeset by Ries Graphics ltd., Milwaukee.
Design: Laurie Shock and Leanne Dillingham.
Map design: Kate Kriege.

2 3 4 5 6 7 8 9 92 91 90 89 88

Children of the World
South Korea

Photography by
Makoto Kubota

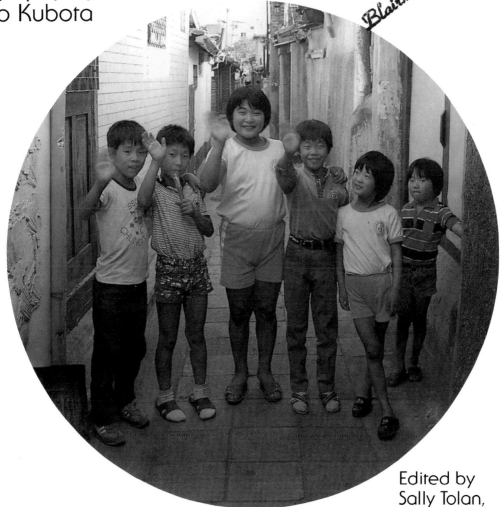

Edited by
Sally Tolan,
MaryLee Knowlton, &
Mark J. Sachner

Gareth Stevens Publishing
Milwaukee

... a note about *Children of the World*:

The children of the world live in fishing towns and urban centers, on islands and in mountain valleys, on sheep ranches and fruit farms. This series follows one child in each country through the pattern of his or her life. Candid photographs show the children with their families, at school, at play, and in their communities. The text describes the dreams of the children and, often through their own words, tells how they see themselves and their lives.

Each book also explores events that are unique to the country in which the child lives, including festivals, religious ceremonies, and national holidays. The *Children of the World* series does more than tell about foreign countries. It introduces the children of each country and shows readers what it is like to be a child in that country.

... and about *South Korea*:

A son of a martial arts instructor, Jyung Ho lives in Seoul, the capital of South Korea. The prospect of the 1988 Olympic Games is exciting to this eleven-year-old boy who prepares for a career as an athlete. In the meantime, he studies English, Japanese, and Korean in school and grows and plays with his friends.

To enhance this book's value in libraries and classrooms, comprehensive reference sections include up-to-date data about South Korea's geography, demographics, language, currency, education, culture, industry, and natural resources. *South Korea* also features a bibliography, research topics, activity projects, and discussions of such subjects as Seoul, the country's history, political system, ethnic and religious composition, and language.

The living conditions and experiences of children in South Korea vary tremendously according to economic, environmental, and ethnic circumstances. The reference sections help bring to life for young readers the diversity and richness of the culture and heritage of the Republic of Korea. Of particular interest are discussions of South Korea's ethnic and cultural heritage and of its situation in the world today, particularly its internal political climate and its relations with the Democratic People's Republic of Korea in the North.

CONTENTS

Roof tops in Seoul.

LIVING IN SOUTH KOREA:
Jyung Ho, a Young Martial Artist

Bae Jyung Ho (also spelled Chung Ho) is an eleven-year-old Korean boy. He lives with his father (a martial arts instructor), his mother, and his two brothers in Seoul, the capital of South Korea. About 9,500,000 people, a quarter of the South Korean population, live in Seoul.

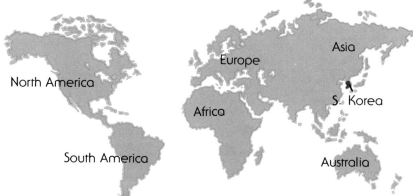

North America

South America

Europe

Asia

Africa

S. Korea

Australia

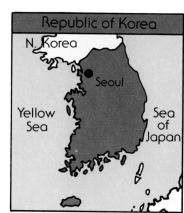

Republic of Korea

N. Korea

Seoul

Yellow Sea

Sea of Japan

After World War II ended in 1945, some countries were divided into two different countries even though they had been unified before the war. Even now, more than 40 years after the war, these countries are divided. In each of them one nationality with one language is split up in two different countries. One of these divided countries is East and West Germany. The other is North and South Korea. South Korea is in the southern part of the Korean Peninsula, in the far eastern part of Asia.

Jyung Ho and his family: Jyung Ho's mother, Jyung Ho, his younger brother Seo Ho, his older brother Joo Ho, and his father.

Jyung Ho and His Family

Jyung Ho is in the 5th grade. Seo Ho is in the 2nd grade, and Joo Ho is in the first year of junior high. Even though they are different ages, they do many things together. They all sleep and study in the same room. After school, they take lessons in *Taekwondo*, a Korean form of karate. They even get the same allowances — 20,000 *won,* or about $25, a month. This is a lot of pocket money for Korean children. Jyung Ho spends most of his money on snacks.

Jyung Ho holding his treasured stuffed animals.

The boys and their father play *yut,* a four-stick game similar to backgammon.

The Bae children watch TV with their friend Namm Il. There are five channels: three of the Korean Broadcasting System, one for the commercial network, and an English-language channel for US soldiers in Korea. All Korean channels broadcast in the evenings only.

Meals are important to the family. Their mother cooks many kinds of food every day. Sometimes their father cannot be home for dinner because of his job running a body-building gym. But he tries to eat with his family as often as he can. Sometimes he takes his sons to a restaurant in Lotte Department Store, the biggest store in Seoul.

After dinner Jyung Ho and his brothers sometimes watch TV with their parents. But most nights they have homework to do until about nine o'clock. And at ten o'clock they are all in bed.

Hodori, another member of the Bae family. *Hodori*, which means "little tiger," is a friendly term for a boy.

안
녕
하
십
니
까

"Hello!"

Jyung Ho and his family at supper. Tonight's menu: beef and radish soup, beans with rice, sheets of dried seaweed, fish boiled in broth, short-necked clams, tofu (bean curd), potato salad, fish cooked in soy sauce and sugar, *pulkogi* (seasoned, barbequed beef), and *kimchi* made from Chinese cabbage. Koreans eat rice and soup with a spoon and the other food with metal, wooden, or bamboo chopsticks.

11

The Bae brothers study in their room.

Koreans introduced Chinese characters thousands of years ago. But about 500 years ago they started a writing system for their own language — Hangŭl. Today Koreans use Hangŭl for most of their writing, and they use Chinese characters mainly for names of people and places.

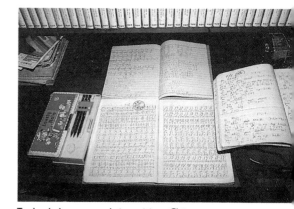

Today's homework is writing Chinese characters.

Jyung Ho's full name is Bae Jyung Ho. Bae is his family name, and Jyung Ho is his given name. His name is written in Hangŭl as " 배정호 ." Here are the other names of Jyung Ho's family: Bae Jyung Man (Jyung Ho's father), Lee Byum Ho (Jyung Ho's mother), Bae Joo Ho (his older brother), and Bae Seo Ho (his younger brother).

You can see that only the mother's family name is different from the others. In Korea women keep their family names when they marry. The children take their father's family name.

The books on the shelf above Jyung Ho's desk are a set of biographies of famous people of the world.

Like most Koreans, Jyung Ho and his brothers sleep on sleeping pads on the floor. When they come into their house they take off their shoes. The stone floor is smooth because it is covered with varnished oil paper. In summer it feels cool to the boys' bare feet. In winter the floor is warm and comfortable when the *ondol* is lit. The ondol is a system of under-floor heating. It is necessary because sometimes the temperature gets down to 0° F, or −15° C.

The boys at the piano, which is one of their mother's family treasures.

13

Every day the three Bae brothers take Hodori for a walk around their neighborhood.

Living in Seoul

Korean houses have many rows of grooves under the floor for their ondols. Large coal briquets are burned at the opening of each groove and warm the floors. A briquet lasts up to 12 hours, so people have to replace them only twice a day — in the morning and evening. If you walk through the city on a winter morning, you can see piles of briquet ashes at the corners of houses.

Seoul is an old city, but its appearance is becoming more and more modern. During the Korean War. in the 1950s, many old buildings were destroyed. Modern buildings have replaced them. Some streets have been widened, and a subway system has been built. Seoul has become more and more modern in preparation for the 1988 Olympic Games.

Jyung Ho's house is in an old neighborhood. It has many old houses and twisting lanes too narrow for cars to pass through. Carts carrying heaps of briquets come and go. Peddlers load their bicycles with fish and vegetables.

For Jyung Ho this neighborhood is like a playground. He hopes that it will not lose its maze of lanes and quaint old houses and turn modern as many Seoul neighborhoods have.

This beautiful door is inside a little courtyard like those of many Korean houses in old neighborhoods.

People are getting ready for winter. Red peppers dry in the sunshine.

The old and new in Seoul.

The Food of Seoul

In Seoul, there are many food stalls, or little outdoor food shops. Some are scattered throughout the city. Many are at large and famous markets, like the East Gate Market. If you were there you could buy cuttlefish (dried or deep-fried), potatoes, baked chestnuts, noodles, fruits and vegetables, or rice porridge with red beans. Or you could buy American foods like donuts or hamburgers. Jyung Ho's favorite food is fried chicken. Today in Seoul there are modern supermarkets, too.

This fruit shop is open from early morning until late at night. You can buy just one piece of fruit if that's all you want.

A very popular food in Korea is *kimchi*, a kind of pickle. It is made by combining a vegetable with spices and other strong-flavored foods. Korean families have their own recipes. The most popular vegetables used in making kimchi are radishes, leeks, cucumbers, turnips, cabbages (especially Chinese cabbages), and Chinese parsley. The spices added might be red pepper, garlic, or sesame. Sometimes people add apples, pears, and other fruit or shellfish like shrimp or crab, or salted fish guts.

Food sellers at their stalls in Seoul's East Gate Market.

Most of the market sellers are women. They open their shops wherever there is space and even in wintry weather.

Every year around the end of November, Jyung Ho's mother begins to make kimchi from Chinese cabbage. One winter she pickled 100 cabbages. Friends and neighbors help her with this big job. She also makes soy sauce and bean paste. Both of these are important ingredients in Korean cooking. She stores these foods in earthenware crocks. These crocks come in various sizes, and Jyung Ho's mother keeps them in the garden.

20

Around the end of November the markets are filled with heaps of Chinese cabbages. People buy them to make kimchi.

People often store their kimchi in large crocks sunk into the ground.

Red pepper in various forms.

Pigs' heads.

An old woman selling baked chestnuts and dried cuttlefish.

A young man selling salted and dried fish.

Rice cakes with bean-jam and bean-rice cakes.

All of these foods can be used in kimchi.

These are also ingredients for kimchi.

Most signs are written in Hangŭl.

A hardware shop.

Fish hung to dry.

A clothing shop.

Heaps of garlic.

A stall selling meat buns and bean-jam b

An assortment of vegetables, spices, fruits, and seafood — all for making kimchi.

Denjang chige (a bean-paste-flavored stew).

Fried fish.

Beef ribs with many seasonings.

Breakfast foods.

Cooked vegetables.

Cold noodles.

Baked fish and denjang chige.

Jyung Ho, Joo Ho, Seo Ho, and Jyung Man eating steamed wonton in a restaurant.

Various kinds of rice cakes.
Noodle and egg dishes.

Bibimbap (rice mixed with other foods).
Raw shellfish with red pepper.

Raw flat fish and octopus.

Kimbap (rice rolled in seaweed).

Fish and seafood chowder.

Raw garlic cloves on seasoned shellfish.

Kimbap and gelidium jelly.

Steamed wonton.

Cooked meat and vegetables.

Kimchi.

Butter-fried vegetables, and buckwheat crepes.

Hand-made noodles in soup.

Pulkogi (seasoned cooked beef).

Wonton in soup.

Children outside their school. Their running shoes are an American brand, but they are made in South Korea.

Jyung Ho and Seo Ho on their way to school with their friends. It takes them five minutes to walk to school.

Kyodong Elementary School

In South Korea an elementary school has six grades. Even though classes don't start until nine, Jyung Ho leaves for school around eight with Seo Ho and his friends Nam Il and Yoon Ping. They play until school starts.

Kyodong Elementary School is 90 years old. It is one of the oldest schools in Seoul. When Japan ruled Korea from 1910 until World War II ended in 1945, many Japanese people lived in Korea. At school, Korean children were taught in the same way that Japanese children were. They used Japanese textbooks. They had to speak Japanese in school and in public, although they could use Korean at home. They were forced to take Japanese names even though they had their own Korean names.

The children at the gate of Kyodong Elementary School.

The principal of Jyung Ho's school was taught by Japanese teachers. He still speaks Japanese well, but he is glad that Korean children learn in their own language today. And he is glad that Japan no longer rules Korea. Still, he thinks Japan and South Korea should try to understand each other better and be friendly neighbors.

About 1800 children attend the Kyodong School, near the center of Seoul. The 5th grade has four classes. Jyung Ho's class has 54 students. Each class period lasts forty minutes, with a 10-minute break between periods. There are six class periods a day. School is over at 3:00 p.m.

The children at their desks. The stove in the middle of the classroom uses briquets to keep the room warm.

First period is Korean language class. Today the students learned several new Chinese characters. For 30 years after Korea's independence from Japan, only the Hangŭl alphabet was taught in schools. But now children are learning Chinese characters too. For homework they will learn the order of characters and practice writing them.

These children look ready for recess. They do not wear uniforms to school.

Jyung Ho's English class with Mr. Park.

The second period is English class. Usually, South Korean children begin studying English in junior high school. But in Jyung Ho's school, the 5th graders have an English class once a week to introduce them to the language. They do not use textbooks. Sometimes they copy what the teacher has written. Other times they read English sentences after the teacher.

Some pupils are learning to use a computer.

Other subjects the 5th graders learn are mathematics, science, social studies, music, art, home economics, and physical education. Jyung Ho's favorite class is physical education. He likes to exercise.

Jyung Ho raises his hand to ask a question.

Some of the girls entertain the class at the Christmas party.

Christmas is coming soon. Today there is a Christmas party during the third and fourth periods at school. The children have brought snacks from home. Each pupil gives part of a favorite snack to their teacher, Mr. Park. Soon Mr. Park's desk is covered with chocolates and cookies. Jyung Ho has brought Mr. Park some grape wine that his mother made. Last night she poured it from a big jar into a bottle for him to take to school.

During the party the children eat their snacks and sing songs. The girls dance and present skits. The boys stick to eating. Some of the girls belong to the school's folk dancing club. They each wear a beautiful costume, called *Chima Jeukori*. When they twirl, their skirts billow out.

The students help keep the classroom clean. Every day some of them have cleaning duty. They also take turns helping serve lunch.

The folk dancing club members in their costumes.

Mr. Park and the boys in the classroom after clean-up duty.

Students serving lunch to their
schoolmates.

Lunch hour comes after the fourth period. There is rice on
Tuesday and Friday and rice cakes or bread on Monday,
Wednesday, and Thursday. The menu today is *tokbokki* (rice
cake seasoned with red pepper), fried wonton, milk, and
mandarin oranges.

In Jyung Ho's school the children can decide whether they will
bring their lunches from home or eat the school lunch.
Sometimes Jyung Ho eats the school lunch. But usually he likes
to bring his lunch. The lunch his mother fixes for him is
delicious, and there is always plenty of it.

Today Jyung Ho's lunch box is full of rice. But the fried wonton
on the school lunch looks delicious. So he reaches over to a
friend's plate with his chopsticks. He is not the only one trading
what he brought from home for a bit of the school lunch.

After school, Jyung Ho sometimes plays at the school playground before he goes home. Often he stops to buy a snack at one of the stalls which stand in a row in front of the school gate. He can buy a big fried wonton or sweet and sour rice rolled in seaweed for about 100 won (fifteen cents).

School children having fried wonton at a food stall.

Jyung Ho and his classmates enjoying their snacks at the Christmas party.

Children in front of a shop that sells plastic models.

Two boys playing Korean chess.

Girls eating snacks at the stall outside the school gate.

On the Way Home from School

After he gets home, he takes his dog for a walk. After that he sometimes goes to a book rental shop and looks for a book to take home and read. The book rental store is a meeting place for boys and girls. Snacks are also sold there. Most of the rental books are comics. The rent is 200 won (about thirty cents) a day. There are also book stores that sell comics. The most popular comics tell about sports like baseball and soccer. Once in a while Jyung Ho stops in at a plastic-model shop or a stationery store. Some days he and his friends play baseball in a sports field near his house. Sometimes they play *janggi* (Korean chess) or other games at home.

Students in a book rental shop.

Books displayed in the school library.

The covers of new comic books paper the windows of a book store.

Jyung Ho and his father and brothers in a game arcade.

Near Jyung Ho's house and next to the sports field is Changdokkung, an old palace. Every evening at five, the South Korean flag at Changdokkung is lowered and the national anthem is played over a loudspeaker. During the anthem, everyone must stand still and face the flag. So when Jyung Ho and his friends are playing there, they stop, hold their hands on their chests, and watch the flag being lowered.

Around the end of September the rice begins to ripen and the roadsides are lined with pink and white cosmos flowers.

Jyung Ho's Cousins in Chunchŏn

If you take a train heading northeast from Seoul, you'll see fewer and fewer houses and more and more fields and meadows out the window. In about an hour and a half, the train arrives at Chunchŏn, where Jyung Ho's cousins, the Oh family, live. Chunchŏn's population is around 170,000. It is the capital of the Kangwon province of South Korea. Beautiful mountains surround Chunchŏn. You can ride in a bus from the center of town to farmland in only fifteen minutes.

The main crops around Chunchŏn are rice and vegetables. Farmers plant rice in early summer and harvest it in autumn. The Oh family lives in a farmhouse near Chunchŏn. The only way they make their living is by farming, and country life seems to suit them fine. The Oh children walk about a half mile to school every day. Their porch is a place to gather and relax, and they have lots of room to play in the country. A bicycle adds to the fun.

The children take turns riding the bicycle.

Some girls have a chat on the Oh's farmhouse porch. The women have taken off their shoes.

The farmhouse has a large courtyard. Clothes are hung there to dry. During the day the family's sleeping pads and quilts are stored in a beautiful cupboard decorated with mother-of-pearl.

The Oh family at the dinner table.

The Oh children walk to school.

Sleeping pads and quilts stored in a decorated cupboard.

The courtyard of a typical Korean home.

Life Near the 38th Parallel

In the southern part of South Korea, you would see many old farmhouses with thatched roofs. But this is in the northern part of South Korea, and here the houses are newer. One reason is that South Korea began a program to modernize farms in the 1970s. New houses have been built around Chunchŏn, and new farm machines and farming techniques have been introduced. But many farmers still use animals to do farm work. Cattle are used to plow the rice paddies and vegetable fields. Farmers use cow manure for fertilizer.

There is another reason for the newer houses. Many of the old houses were damaged badly in the Korean War, which started in 1950 and lasted three years. Many of the buildings around here have been rebuilt. Chunchŏn is very close to the 38th parallel, which divides North Korea from South Korea.

A farmer leads his cow along a village lane.

North Korea is allied with the Soviet Union. South Korea is allied with the United States. The Koreans are one people, but they have been divided into two nations. They have two different political systems. People of North and South Korea cannot go freely to the other nation. Many families have been separated. Both governments have been talking about letting family members write, telephone, or visit one another.

Whenever Jyung Ho travels to the countryside, he thinks about what Korea might have been like as one nation, and what it might be like someday.

Jyung Ho, his father, Seo Ho, and Joo Ho at the Taekwondo hall.

Sports: Hard Work and Play

Back in Seoul, Jyung Ho practices his Taekwondo. He hopes to be a Taekwondo expert when he grows up. Like Japanese karate, Taekwondo is a form of self-protection.

Jyung Ho goes to a Taekwondo hall at five o'clock every afternoon and trains for an hour. It is tiring work, but it is very popular with Korean boys. There are many Taekwondo halls in Seoul. Jyung Ho's father often comes to check on his sons' progress. He holds fifth rank in Taekwondo and is a martial arts instructor.

Jyung Ho practicing a kick.

Joo Ho, Jyung Ho, their father, and Seo Ho at the public bath.

Baseball and soccer are also popular in Korea. A few years ago professional baseball leagues were begun. Like North Americans, South Korean children idolize their baseball heroes.

The whole Bae family is looking forward to their winter vacation. It lasts from the middle of December until the beginning of February. They are going skiing. This will be the first time on skis for the boys.

The family also enjoys bathing and relaxing at the public baths. Some families in South Korea still do not have bath tubs or showers at home. So they go to the public baths when they want to bathe. The public bath that Jyung Ho and his family use is open from 7:00 a.m. to 9:00 p.m. There is a separate section for women and girls and one for men and boys.

Jyung Ho and Seo Ho give their parents a formal New Year's greeting.

New Year's Day — A Big Holiday

Like most traditional Korean holidays, New Year's Day is celebrated according to the lunar, or Chinese, calendar. So it does not fall on the same day every year by our Western calendar. New Year's Day is often in the cold winter months.

Like most South Koreans, Jyung Ho's family dresses up for New Year's Day in bright Korean folk costumes. The boys give their parents a formal New Year's bow. After that they get their New Year's gift and eat *ddeuk guk* (soup with rice cakes).

Dressed up for New Year's Day. Joo Ho is missing from the photo because he is at a friend's house.

They go outside to take New Year's pictures. It is cold — about 15°F or − 10°C. Usually in South Korean winters, three cold days are followed by four warmer days. Finally the coldness disappears and spring comes. The spring school term starts at the beginning of March. Jyung Ho will soon be in the 6th grade. He looks forward to a good year.

Two girls in colorful New Year's costumes.

The city of Seoul at sunset. New skyscraper apartment buildings have been built across the river from downtown. They house about 50,000 people.

46

47

FOR YOUR INFORMATION: South Korea

Official Name: *Taehan Min-guk*   Republic of Korea
(tie-HAHN min-GUK)

Capital: Seoul

History

Ancient Korea

The modern Republic of Korea was founded in 1948. But Korea has a very long history. One legend tells that Korea was founded around 2400 BC by Tan-Gun, the son of a god, and a woman of the Bear clan. People call the Korea of that era Ancient Choson. That kingdom lasted for 1200 years, but it later split into different parts.

Korea is very close to China, and some areas of Ancient Choson later became part of China. The clans that descended from the people of Ancient Choson eventually merged into three kingdoms: Koguryo, Paekche, and Silla. Koguryo fought with kingdoms of China. But Silla had help from the Tang kingdom of China and finally took over the whole Korean Peninsula. Some soldiers from Koguryo took an army to China and established a kingdom there. The kingdom was called Parhae in what is now known as Manchuria. Much later, when other armies conquered that area, the ruling group from Parhae came back to the Korean Peninsula.

The Silla Kingdom

The United Silla Kingdom reached its peak in the 8th century AD. During this period, Buddhism became strong. The Buddhists built a great temple and a shrine and began printing their scriptures with wood blocks. There was wealth and increasing scholarship — even an astronomical observatory — in the Silla Kingdom. But in the 9th century, amidst rebellion and fighting, the unified Silla Kingdom was overthrown and broken up.

The Koryo Kingdom

What was once Silla became the Koryo Kingdom. This new name is the origin of *Korea*. The Kingdom of Koryo lasted until 1392 AD. During its era, slaves were freed. Confucianism gained power and influenced the form of government. At one time many Buddhist books were lost in a fire. It would have been too costly to replace them by using wood blocks to print them. So movable metal type was invented, and printing changed forever. Histories of the kingdoms were compiled. But there was conflict in the kingdom. And there were invasions, first by the Mongol tribes from China and later by Japanese pirates.

The Choson Kingdom

48   At the end of the 14th century, the Koryo Kingdom ended and the Choson

Kingdom began. In the West it is called the Yi Dynasty. This kingdom lasted until 1910. Its greatest ruler was King Sejong (1418-1450). He studied science, music, medicine, Confucianism, and language. Under his rule scholars received encouragement and support. Printing was improved, and the Hangŭl alphabet was developed. The rain gauge was invented to help farmers. King Sejong promoted astronomy, musical notation, and the publication of medical information. He also improved the land tax system.

During much of its history, Korea has been pressured, fought over, and even invaded by neighboring countries. Japan invaded Korea twice in the 1590s, and China attacked in 1627. Finally, the Yi Dynasty kings set a "closed door" policy to protect their country from outsiders. Korea became known as the "Hermit Kingdom." But Korea continued to show respect to China's rulers.

Japanese Occupation

In the late 19th and early 20th centuries, Christian missionaries and traders from the West entered Korea. China, Russia, and Japan were fighting for control of northeast Asia. Japan won and in 1910 occupied Korea. Japan tried to suppress the Korean language and culture and make Korea Japanese. Korea was under strict Japanese control until the end of World War II in 1945.

A Divided Korea

When World War II ended, the USSR controlled the northern part of Korea, and the US controlled the southern part. The dividing line was the 38th parallel. It was supposed to be a temporary division. The United Nations was to supervise elections in all Korea. But North Korea refused to have these elections. So they were held just in South Korea. Syngman Rhee was elected president. Unfortunately, he proved to be a dictator, and people eventually rebelled against him.

A theater in Seoul showing Korean movies. South Korea has become quite Westernized since World War II, and many movies come from Hollywood. But South Korea also has its own expanding film industry.

The Korean War

In 1949 US troops withdrew from Korea. In 1950 the People's Democratic Republic of Korea, or North Korea, invaded the Republic of Korea, or South Korea. Their goal was to unify all of Korea under communism and to keep US troops out of the South.

United Nations troops, including many from the US, Canada, and other Western nations, fought to drive the North Koreans out of South Korea. It was a bitter war. 49

Many soldiers and civilians were killed in the fighting and bombing by both sides. Chinese troops entered the war to help the North Koreans. UN troops fought to drive them out of South Korea. Finally there were peace talks. A treaty was signed in July, 1953. Korea was still divided, now at the demilitarized zone (DMZ) near the 38th parallel.

The division continues today. Families, friends, or people wanting to do business cannot travel freely back and forth. The Red Cross has tried to help with this problem. The two governments have talked about reuniting Korea. But the talks have not succeeded so far. There are serious differences in how the two Koreas run their countries. North Korea is a communist country and is allied with the USSR and China. It is opposed to capitalism. South Korea is a capitalistic country and is allied with the US and to an increasing degree with Japan. It is opposed to communism.

Because they fear one another, both Koreas spend much of their income on armies and weapons. If they are to become one nation again, or even to live in peace as neighbors, they will have to make some compromises. Some people in both countries do not think that reunification is possible.

Revolutions and Progress

Since the war, South Korea has had many problems. People were not satisfied with President Rhee's dictatorial government, and when elections came, the president's people tried to win them unfairly. Finally, the protests were so strong that in 1960 President Rhee resigned.

The new government was not a dictatorship, but it was not strong enough to solve the country's many problems. In 1961, military leaders took over the government. The new president was General Park Chung Hee. The South Korean economy and society improved under President Park's leadership. Korea adopted a new constitution. But President Park had the powers of a dictator. He was assassinated in 1979.

A year later Chun Doo Hwan became president. There is now another new constitution. Korea has had strong economic growth under his rule. But some people think that President Chun has too much power and does not give the people enough freedom.

Population and Ethnic Groups

More than 40,000,000 people live in South Korea. Most of them are descended from the tribes that came to the Korean Peninsula thousands of years ago. Koreans are racially related to the Japanese, Chinese, and other Mongoloid, or Asiatic, peoples. Over the centuries, however, Koreans have developed their own identity as a race and as a national people, although there are some Chinese people living in the large cities.

Religion

Many of the world's great religions have followers in Korea. About 20% of the people are Buddhists. Buddhism is an ancient Eastern religion which teaches that one is born again and again until he or she reaches spiritual perfection. Buddha, its founder, taught that we become better by giving up worldly possessions and pleasures. There are beautiful temples to Buddha, some way off in the mountains. Some Buddhists become monks. They devote their lives to prayer.

Another 20% of South Koreans are Christian. Some are Catholic, but more are Protestant. There are 5,000,000 Presbyterian Protestants in South Korea.

A church program on Christmas Eve. About 20% of South Korea is Christian.

Some people do not consider the teachings of Confucius a formal religion. But the rules of Confucianism have a strong effect on the way many Koreans live. Confucianism teaches loyalty to leaders and to parents and other family members. It also teaches respect for ancestors. It holds education to be very important.

In ancient times Korean people believed that spirits lived in trees and mountains, animals and rivers, and other parts of nature. They believed that people must please these spirits. Today most Koreans consider this belief, called *Shamanism*, superstitious. But many of its ideas and symbols linger on, especially in rural areas.

Government

The Republic of Korea adopted its first constitution in 1948. The constitution was changed eight times between 1948 and 1987. Under the present constitution, the president is elected by an electoral college. Many in Korea are calling for direct election of the president by the people. They believe that the president can too easily control the electoral college. Even though the constitution limits the president to one seven-year term, he can use the electoral college to keep his supporters in power.

The legislature is called the National Assembly. Two-thirds of its members are elected directly by the voters. The other members are chosen by the ruling party. Many people in South Korea want all the Assembly members to be directly elected by the voters. The legislature's duties are to pass or reject laws and treaties, inspect the national budget accounts, and agree to the declaration of war or peace.

The president appoints the Chief Justice of the Supreme Court with the approval of the National Assembly. He also appoints the other Supreme Court justices with the Chief Justice's approval. The Chief Justice appoints the judges of the lower courts. 51

Under the constitution the courts are supposed to be independent of the executive and legislative branches of the government. Some critics of the government feel that the courts favor the government over individual citizens.

The constitution guarantees human rights, but critics of the government say that human rights are often abused. The government often arrests and jails its opponents. Students demonstrating to protest against government abuses have been shot by police. The government says it is necessary to rule South Korea strictly because of the threat of possible invasion from North Korea. But some experts say opposition *within* the country to harsh rule is a greater danger. Many who oppose the present government blame the US for supporting it.

South Korea's army and police force are large and powerful. They support the government, and it is unlikely that they will let the opposition move into power if President Chun wants to keep control at the end of his term.

Language

Koreans speak the Korean language. A member of the Altaic family of languages, Korean is related to Manchurian and Mongolian. It is not related to Chinese, but it has borrowed many words from Chinese because of the closeness of the two countries. Centuries ago Koreans wrote their language in Chinese characters. But in the 15th century King Sejong developed the Hangŭl alphabet. It is a very scientific alphabet and is used all over Korea. Chinese characters are still used for some names.

Art and Music

Koreans have great love for the arts. The world is discovering that Korea has a long and noble artistic history. In 1979 and the early 1980s an exhibit entitled "5000 Years of Korean Art" traveled to many great cities in the world.

In Seoul the National Museum shows paintings and sculpture from many eras of Korean art. The government has put out a list of National Treasures: buildings, paintings, dances, antique handcrafts, music, and so on. The Korean people revere and protect these treasures.

Painting is an ancient art in Korea. The oldest Buddhist painting in the world is Korean. Calligraphy (brush writing) is considered as important an art as painting. Often painting and calligraphy will appear on the same canvas or paper. In recent years Western ideas and methods have influenced South Korean painting.

Sculpture in Korea was an important part of the Buddhist tradition. Large statues of Buddha are admired for their beauty and simplicity. At the famous grotto, *Sokkuran,* near Kyongju is a great sculptured Buddhist monument. Most of Korea's sculpture has been done in stone, but there are also bronze, wood, and clay sculptures.

Korea is also famous for its ceramics. Archaeologists have found ceramics from prehistoric times. During the Koryo period artisans made the beautiful pottery known as celadon. It is famous for its thin green glaze and decorative designs. The Yi Dynasty's punchong pottery and white-glazed pottery are famous, too.

There are two kinds of traditional music and dance in Korea. Court music and dance are slow and dignified. Musicians play ancient instruments. Folk music and dance have faster tempos. They are more energetic. The roots of folk music and dance are in the land and the lives of country people.

Some poetry is closely connected to music. *Shijo* are short lyric poems that used to be sung. Today they are written to be read. In the old days traveling minstrels used to chant stories and play drums. Today the literature of the West has influenced the writing and theater of Korea. But Koreans still enjoy their traditional mask-dance drama.

Education

Koreans value education highly. South Korean children must attend elementary school (1st through 6th grades). Ninety percent of Korean young people attend high school. The high school course is three years.

Students take government-run examinations to be admitted to colleges. Today colleges offer more technical educations than in the past to help their graduates find work in Korea's growing industrial economy.

During the Japanese occupation, the Korean language and culture were suppressed in the schools. When the Japanese left after World War II, South Korea started developing its own educational system. But between 1950 and 1953, the Korean War destroyed or damaged many schools and interrupted the education of thousands of children.

Since then South Korea has worked hard to build a strong educational system. The government provides free education to students from 1st grade through high school. It controls much of the content of that education. It also supports many college students who cannot afford to pay tuition. Beyond high school and college South Koreans can continue their education by using educational television.

Industry, Agriculture, and Natural Resources

Natural Resources

South Korea does not have rich natural resources. The country imports its oil, but is searching for sources in the country and offshore. Ores found in South Korea include iron, tungsten, silver, kaolin (a source of aluminum), lead, and zinc. There are also deposits of anthracite coal and limestone. However, mining accounts for only about one percent of the nation's production.

The government has put strict controls on tree cutting. Foresters are planting new trees and protecting older ones. They are developing pest-and-disease-resistant types. The reforestation program is helping to reduce flooding and soil erosion.

Agriculture

Because so much of Korea is mountainous, only 22% of the land can be farmed. And many people who used to farm now live and work in the cities. Still, food production has improved in South Korea, in large part because of irrigation and mechanization in farming. The country now produces enough rice to feed its people.

Briquets like these are the most commonly used fuel in Korea. Unlike briquets used for cooking in North America that are made of charcoal, these are actually manufactured out of coal.

Besides rice, grain crops are barley, soybeans, and corn. Fruits such as apples, pears, peaches, and persimmons are also grown. The use of plastic greenhouses has increased production of vegetables such as cabbage, turnips, and radishes. Livestock production is growing. Draft and dairy cattle, pigs, and chickens are increasing in number on farms.

A rural development program called *Saemaul Undung* (New Community Movement) started in 1971. Better housing, improved roads and water supplies, and expanded electrification are making life easier for people in the villages. Local industries operate to give work to farmers in the off-season.

Industry

South Korea's industry has grown rapidly in recent years. The nation has become an exporter of industrial products to North America, Europe, Asia, and Africa. South Korea became the world's tenth largest producer of steel in 1984. South Korean industry also builds ships and produces industrial machinery and equipment, electronic equipment like television sets and computers and VCRs, and cars and trucks and buses. The petrochemical industry is new in Korea. It makes plastics and synthetic rubber, refines oil, and produces chemical fertilizers and pesticides. The textile industry is one of the oldest in Korea and produces cotton, wool, and synthetic fabrics.

Other products of South Korea are cement, processed foods, leather goods, plywood, paper and paper products, soap, tires, farm equipment, and sewing machines.

South Korea has expanded its construction industry to include overseas work. Because it has to import oil, the country is building nuclear power plants. In its industrial growth, South Korea has been assisted by both Japan and the United

States. But its people are well-educated, work hard, and respect the authority of their employers. The have worked long hours at low wages. This has helped the growth of the South Korean economy. But workers want to be better paid. So there are likely to be demands from labor.

Another problem that faces the South Korean economy is the need to spend large amounts on defense. A third problem is the possibility that the US, as well as other countries to which South Korea exports, may decrease the amount they buy.

Land

North and South Korea cover a 625 mile (1000 km)-long peninsula that is connected to China at its north. Korea's northeasternmost point touches the USSR's southeasternmost point. All its other borders are water. The Yellow Sea, called the West Sea in Korea, is on its west. The Sea of Japan, the East Sea, is on its east. And the Pacific Ocean is at its south. Because Korea is a mountainous land, some have called it the "Switzerland of Asia." Others have named it the "land of the morning calm," because of the beautiful misty mornings in the mountains.

South Korea is in the southern half of the peninsula. It occupies about 38,000 sq miles (99,000 sq km), about the area of Virginia in the US or of the island of Newfoundland in Canada. On its east coast the sea comes up against the steep mountain sides. There are no major harbors on the east coast, but there are a few fine beaches, and the rugged coast is beautiful. There are two principal mountain ranges: the Nangnim range in the north and its southern extension, the Taebaek range. West of these mountains the land slopes down toward the western and southern seas. On the southern and western coasts there are fine harbors and beaches. Because of the high tides, there are wide mud flats along some of the shoreline at low tide.

Many rivers and streams come down from the mountains. The ones that go eastward rush down the steep mountain sides. The rivers going west and south flow more gently. Some of them are dammed and diverted to irrigate farms. The Han, the Kŭm, and the Naktong are major rivers in South Korea.

There are about 3400 islands off the Korean coast. Cheju Island is the largest and best known. Mount Halla on Cheju, an inactive volcano, is the highest peak in South Korea.

Climate

South Korea's climate is temperate. The winters are cold, with temperatures around freezing. Often after three days of cold weather, four warm days will follow. In the southern part of the country the winters are a little milder. The summers are hot and muggy. The rainy season comes in June, July, or August. The weather is most pleasant in spring and fall.

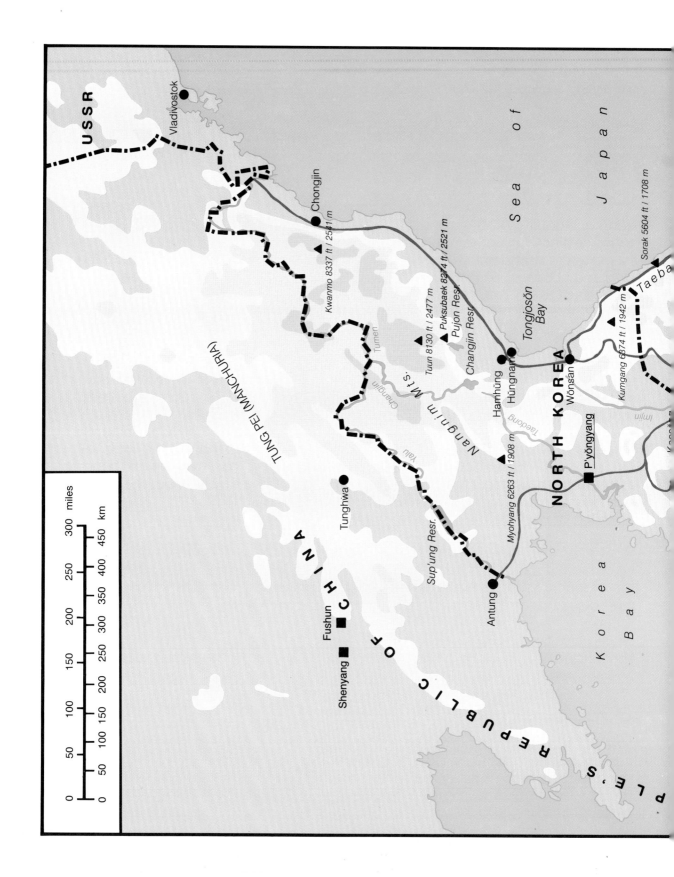

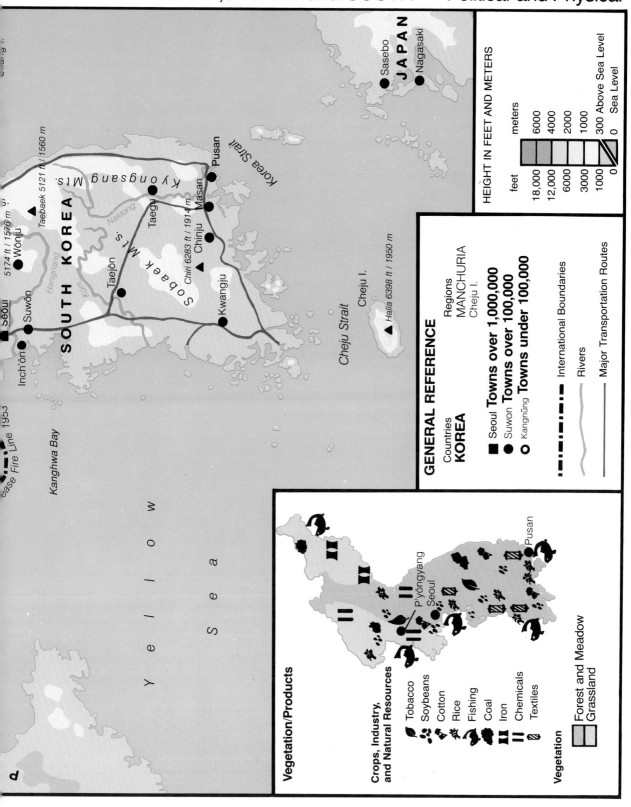

HEIGHT IN FEET AND METERS

feet	meters
18,000	6000
12,000	4000
6000	2000
3000	1000
1000	300 Above Sea Level
0	0 Sea Level

GENERAL REFERENCE

Countries	Regions
KOREA	MANCHURIA
	Cheju I.

■ Seoul Towns over 1,000,000
● Suwon Towns over 100,000
○ Kangnŭng Towns under 100,000

▪▫▪ International Boundaries
〰 Rivers
— Major Transportation Routes

Crops, Industry, and Natural Resources

Tobacco
Soybeans
Cotton
Rice
Fishing
Coal
Iron
Chemicals
Textiles

Vegetation/Products

Vegetation
Forest and Meadow
Grassland

JAPAN
Sasebo
Nagasaki

Pusan
Kyongsang Mts
Masan
Taegu
Chinju
Naktong
Chiri 6283 ft / 1914 m
Kwangju
Sobaek Mts
Taejŏn

SOUTH KOREA
Taebaek 5121 ft / 1560 m
5174 ft / 1576 m
Wŏnju
Hangang
Kŭm
Seoul
Suwŏn
Inch'ŏn

Korea Strait
Cheju Strait
Cheju I.
Halla 6398 ft / 1950 m

Yellow Sea
Kanghwa Bay
Cease Fire Line 1953

P'yongyang
Seoul
Pusan

d

Sports

South Koreans have become very sports-minded in recent years. Athletes, architects, builders, merchants, and government officials worked hard to prepare for the 1988 Olympic Games in Seoul. They built a stadium that seats 100,000 people as well as other sports facilities. Seoul was also the site of the 1986 Asian Games.

Koreans like to watch and participate in many kinds of sports, and South Korean athletes have done well in international competition. Soccer is probably the most popular sport in South Korea. Six professional teams compete in a pennant race every year. Baseball is becoming more and more popular. Not only pro teams, but also high school and college teams take to the diamond. Women and girls as well as men and boys play volleyball and have done well in international competition.

Wrestling has been a traditional Korean form of competition for centuries. *Ssirum* is the ancient Korean form of wrestling. *Taekwondo,* a form of martial arts, developed in Korea 2000 years ago. Today it is common in many other countries. In fact, Korean *Taekwondo* instructors can be found in cities around the world.

Individual sports such as tennis, table tennis, golf, archery, skating, skiing, shooting, boxing, and competitive swimming are also quite popular. In addition to competitive sports South Koreans enjoy hiking, mountain climbing, hunting, and fishing, and just swimming for pleasure.

Seoul

The name *Seoul* means capital, and Seoul has been a Korean capital for almost 600 years. It was founded in 1394, almost 100 years before Columbus' voyage to America, in the early years of the Yi Dynasty.

Seoul is a huge modern city. More than 9,500,000 people live there. Skyscrapers and other modern buildings dominate its profile. Most of them are less than 20 years old. After the Korean War, Seoul was in ruins. These new buildings have replaced buildings that were destroyed in that war. The rebuilding of Seoul continues today. Seoul also has a large and modern subway system.

Seoul has outgrown the wall that once surrounded the old city. But ruins of that wall remain: the great South Gate and East Gate. At both of these gates are large markets where people can buy anything from vegetables and fried fish to blue jeans and transistor radios. Another great gate is called the Gate of Transformation by Light, or *Kwanghwamun* in Korean.

People can also see the past in the palaces that have survived from the period of the Yi Dynasty. Kyongbokung Palace is at the east wall. On the palace grounds are beautiful gardens with lily ponds and pavilions. In one palace building is the National Museum with its collection of art and treasures of past kingdoms. In another is the National Folklore Museum. Here people can see the farm and cooking tools,

Rush hour in Seoul. The taxis and buses nearly outnumber private automobiles — one sign of a large, modern city.

games and toys, dances and costumes of the common folk. Another famous palace is the Toksukung Palace. In one of its buildings is the National Museum of Art. The Changdokkung Palace is also quite well-known. Its 78-acre (195-hectare) Secret Garden, called the *Biwon* in Korean, is a favorite with visitors.

South of the Han River is the new Olympic Stadium, the Olympic Village, and other sports facilities built for the 1988 games. Many bridges span the river. Some have two levels to handle all the rush-hour traffic.

Near the middle of the city is Mt. Namsan. On its slopes are large hotels. The mountain itself is a park, with libraries, a botanical garden, the National Theater, and statues of famous Korean leaders. On top of the mountain is a large hotel and Seoul Tower, from which people can get broad views of the city.

Seoul is a crowded and busy city. Koreans are polite people. Still, they are so used to bumping people and being bumped as they walk in the city that they don't see any need to apologize. Besides being the capital, Seoul is the center of business and culture. It is no wonder everyone is in such a hurry.

Currency

The unit of money in South Korea is the *won*. There are 500, 1000, 5000, and 10,000 won bills. There are 1, 5, 10, 50, 100, and 500 won coins.

Koreans in North America

Emigration from Korea to the United States did not really begin until 1905. In that year many Koreans went to Hawaii to work in sugar and pineapple fields. The work was hard and the pay was poor. But they had left even worse conditions in Korea. There had been a drought and then floods and the rice crop was ruined. There was not enough to eat.

Later, Korean workers went to California to work on fruit farms. Many US workers resented them because they were taking jobs that US workers wanted. In 1924, the government passed an Oriental Exclusion Act to keep Asian workers out of the United States. Under this law the only Oriental people who could enter the United States were those who were attending college. This discriminatory law was canceled during World War II.

These workers were mostly men, and they were lonely. They wanted to marry Korean women. So the system of picture brides developed. The worker would send his picture to a Korean woman and she would agree to marry him. The brides left Korea without permission and without passports. They married on the dock when their ships came in so that they could enter the US on their new husbands' passports.

Many of the early immigrants and their families started small businesses like fruit and vegetable markets and laundries. They saw that their children received good educations. They have become successful citizens.

During World War II the US government did not trust its Japanese-American residents living on the west coast. In an act of great injustice, the government put many of these Americans in internment, or concentration, camps. Many Koreans were also interned simply because they looked Japanese.

After the Korean War, there were many Korean orphans or children whose fathers were American soldiers. Many of these came to the United States to be adopted by American families.

North Koreans are not allowed to emigrate and do not come to North America. But South Koreans continue to arrive. In more recent years the immigrants have been professional or business people instead of the unskilled and semiskilled workers of earlier years. In North America many of them work as doctors, teachers, and merchants. Many have also come to attend colleges and universities.

In 1985 alone, 30,532 South Koreans applied for permanent residence in the US, and 934 in Canada. That same year 12,161 South Koreans applied to enter the US as students, and 683 to enter Canada. In Canada most South Koreans have settled in large cities, especially in Toronto, Montreal, and Vancouver. In fact, two-thirds of all Asians coming to Canada come to those three cities. In the US most South Koreans are in Los Angeles, New York, and Chicago. Koreans like big cities. It is easier to find jobs there and to find other Koreans to be with.

Some South Koreans come here to escape the overcrowding of their own country. Others come because they do not like the political situation in South Korea. Many see North America as a place of economic opportunity.

More Books About Korea

Here are more books about Korea. If you are interested in them, check your library. Some may be helpful in doing research for the "Things to Do" projects that follow.

Korea. McNair (Childrens Press)
The Koreans in America. Patterson/Kim (Lerner)
The Land and People of Korea. Solberg (Lippincott)
North and South Korea (A First Book). Gurney (Franklin Watts)

Glossary of Useful Korean Terms

bibimbap (BIH-bim-bap) . . . . rice mixed with other foods
ddeuk guk (dee-UHK GUHK) . . . . soup with rice cakes
denjang chige (DEN-jang CHEEGE) . . a stew flavored with bean paste
Hangŭl (HAHN-gool) . . . . an alphabet just for the Korean language
hodori (ho-DOOR-i) . . . . "little tiger"; a friendly term for a boy
janggi (JANG-i) . . . . Korean chess game
kimbap . . . . rice rolled in seaweed
kimchi (kim-CHEE) . . . . a dish made by combining cabbage or some other vegetable with spices and other flavorful foods
Ni how (nee how) . . . . Hello (Chinese)
ondola . . . . an under-the-floor heating system
pulkogi (pull-KOHG-i) . . . . seasoned cooked beef
ssirum (SEER-room) . . . . ancient Korean form of wrestling
Taekwondo (tie-KWAHN-doh) . . . . . . a Korean form of karate
tokbokki (tahk-BAHK-i) . . . . rice cake seasoned with red pepper
yut . . . . a four-stick game similar to backgammon

Things to Do — Research Projects

South Korea's economy is growing by leaps and bounds, even in the face of widespread protests by people who feel that the government's domestic policies and tactics are corrupt and repressive. As you read about political, social, and economic developments in South Korea, or any country, keep in mind the importance of current facts. Some of the research projects that follow need accurate, up-to-date information from current sources. Two publications your library may have will tell you about recent newspaper and magazine articles on many topics:

The Reader's Guide to Periodical Literature

Children's Magazine Guide

For accurate answers to questions about such topics of current interest as the South Korean government and its dealings with both its domestic critics and the North, look up *Korea* in these two publications. They will lead you to the most up-to-date information from current sources.

1. Using books in your library, find out more about your country's role in the war that divided North and South Korea.

2. How far is Seoul, South Korea, from where you live? Using maps, travel guides, travel agents, or any other useful resources you know of, find out how you could get there and how long it would take.

3. Choose one of the religions practiced in South Korea and find out more about it. Is it practiced differently in the North? Report what you find to your classmates.

4. Why do you think it is important to study the history of South Korea to understand it? What predictions can you make about its future from what you know about its past?

More Things to Do — Activities

These projects are designed to encourage you to think more about South Korea. They offer ideas for interesting group or individual projects for school or home.

1. Calligraphy, or brush writing, is as much an art in Korea as painting. Find books in your library or bookstore on calligraphy. Try it yourself.

2. See if your town has any people who have come here from South Korea. Invite one or several to your class to talk about the experience of coming to this country.

3. Take a trip to a shopping mall or department store. Look on the labels of clothing, appliances, toys, and other products. What kinds of things can you find that were made in South Korea?

4. If you would like a pen pal in South Korea, write to these people:

International Pen Friends
P.O. Box 65
Brooklyn, New York 11229

Tell them your age and what country you want your pen pal to be from. Also include your full name and address.

Index

Blairmore Municipal Library

This book may be kept until last date stamped below.

A fine of 10 cents per week will be imposed for each week the book is overdue

DEC 9 9f
JAN 3 '92
SEP 18 9 2
OCT 1 0 2
JUL 0 8 2003
2013